# Nature Trail

# Pond

## Jen Green

### Photographs by Emma Solley

WAYLAND

First published in 2010 by Wayland

Copyright © Wayland 2010

Wayland
338 Euston Road
London NW1 3BH

Wayland Australia
Level 17/207 Kent Street
Sydney, NSW 2000

Senior editor: Camilla Lloyd
Designer: Phipps Design
Photographer: Emma Solley
Illustrator: Peter Bull

Picture Acknowledgments:
The author and publisher would like to thank the following for allowing their pictures to be reproduced in this publication:
p.6 Paul Broadbent/ iStockphoto; p.9 (bottom) © David Chapman/Alamy;
p.10 © Mike Lane/Alamy; p.11 (bottom) © blickwinkel/Alamy;
p.15 © David Chapman/ Alamy; p.17 (bottom) © Robert Frith/ iStockphoto;
p.25 (bottom) © WILDLIFE GmbH/Alamy; p.26 © blickwinkel/Alamy.

British Library Cataloguing in Publication Data:
Green, Jen.
Pond. – (Nature trail)
1. Pond ecology–Juvenile literature.
2. Pond animals–Juvenile literature.
3. Pond plants–Juvenile literature.
I. Title II. Series
577.6'36-dc22

ISBN: 978 0 7502 6091 6

Printed in China

Wayland is a division of Hachette Children's Books, an Hachette UK company.
www.hachette.co.uk

# Contents

# At the pond

A pond is a hole or hollow filled with fresh water. Some ponds are made by people. Others form naturally when rainwater fills a hollow. Ponds are full of plants and animals, so they are a brilliant place to study wildlife!

Trees such as willows and alders grow by ponds. They need a lot of water and don't mind their roots getting wet.

Ponds contain still or very slow-moving water. Most are fairly shallow with a muddy bottom.

All animals, including these baby swans or cygnets, need food, water and shelter. Ponds provide all three, so it's no wonder many creatures live here.

This symbol shows when extra care is needed. Always be careful near water and never go alone. Take good care of nature too – don't pick flowers, and treat animals gently.

# On the trail

On the nature trail at the pond you will need a hat, sunglasses, sun cream and wellies.

hat

sunglasses

sun cream

strong shoes or boots

waterproof clothing

Make notes and drawings using a notebook, pen and coloured pencils. A magnifying glass, binoculars, camera, fishing net and a container will come in handy.

magnifying glass

notebook and pen

coloured pencils

fishing net

binoculars

ice cream container

# On the bank

Ponds contain several mini-**habitats**, such as banks, surface waters and the bottom. Each has its own plants and animals. Grass, reeds and flowering plants grow by ponds. Some animals spend their lives on the bank, others just visit to drink.

Water voles live in burrows by the water's edge. These little mammals are quite rare.

These **mammals** visit ponds to drink, and leave their prints in the mud. You may also see the tracks of voles, water shrews and birds.

A fox's prints are similar to those of a dog.

A deer leaves deep, narrow hoof prints.

An otter has large paws with five clawed toes.

Mud can be very slippery! Take extra care by the water's edge.

## What do you see?

Footprints can be used to identify wildlife long after the animals have gone. Compare the prints you find with the ones shown here. Find more prints in a wildlife book or on the Internet.

a fox's footprints

a deer's footprints

an otter's footprints

Ponds vary in size from **millponds** to tiny garden pools like this one.

Dragonflies patrol along the bank, catching insects.

7

# Floating at the surface

Plants such as weeds and water lilies float at the surface. Some insects are so light they can skim across the surface without sinking. Frogs rest on lily pads and wait for passing insects to eat.

Lily leaves and flowers float on water. The long stems reach down to roots buried in the mud.

A lily leaf is called a pad.

Can you tell if the water plants are floating freely or fixed to the bed of the pond?

The pond skater is an insect with long legs and a lightweight body. It slides across the water surface, which acts like a thin skin.

## What do you see?

Use a magnifying glass to study small creatures at the surface. Make notes and sketches of what you see. Loud noises and sudden movements will frighten animals. The quieter you are, the more you will see!

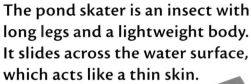

When an insect comes within range, the frog shoots out its long, sticky tongue.

Frogs have strong legs for swimming and leaping.

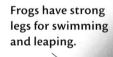

# Below the surface

Many kinds of minibeasts live just below the surface. Like all animals, they need to breathe **oxygen**. Some take air from the surface. Some carry a bubble of air down with them. Others take oxygen from the water using **gills**, as fish do.

The water scorpion breathes air at the surface using the long, thin tube on its tail.

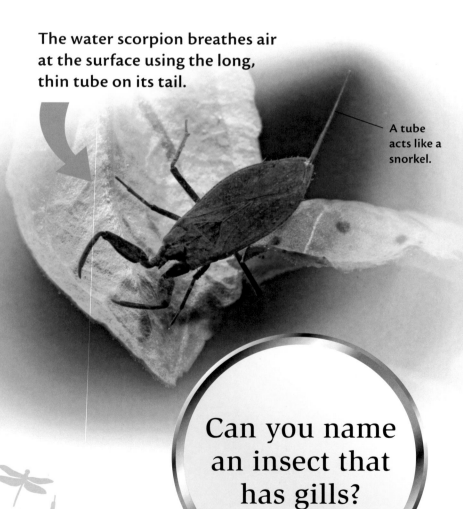

A tube acts like a snorkel.

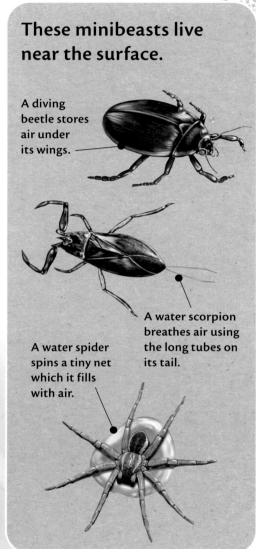

**These minibeasts live near the surface.**

A diving beetle stores air under its wings.

A water scorpion breathes air using the long tubes on its tail.

A water spider spins a tiny net which it fills with air.

Can you name an insect that has gills?

⚠ Take care when handling pond creatures. They are delicate and some can bite.

feeler

foot

Pond snails swim about using their soft, rubbery foot. The long feelers are for sensing.

feathery gill

Mayfly are insects whose young grow up in water. Young mayflies, called **larvae**, breathe using three feathery gills on their tails.

## What do you see?

Fill a container with pond water. Sweep your net gently across the surface. Empty it into the container. Study the creatures you have caught with a magnifying glass. Then return them to the pond.

# On stones and plants

Ponds contain all sorts of minibeasts. Shrimps and worms lurk under stones or in the mud. Snails crawl over plants. Some of these small creatures are plant-eaters, others are meat-eating **predators**.

Pond snails feed on tiny plants which they scrape off rocks. They creep along on their muscular foot.

foot

Garden snails also like wet places and visit ponds to feed on plants.

The hard shell protects the snail's soft body.

feeler

Crane flies have long, thin legs and bodies. We call them daddy-long-legs.

These creepers and crawlers live on plants and stones.

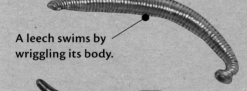

A leech swims by wriggling its body.

A flatworm is a distant cousin of the leech.

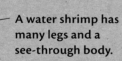

A water shrimp has many legs and a see-through body.

A young caddisfly lives in a silk case. It sticks stones and twigs to the outside as a disguise.

## What do you see?

Sweep your net along the bottom. Empty the contents into a container filled with pond water. You can also lift up stones to find lurking creatures. Try to group the minibeasts you find under these headings:

- Insects
- Worms
- Shrimps
- Snails

# In deep water

Fish, frogs and newts lurk in deep water. These skilled swimmers dive down to find food or hide from enemies. Frogs, toads and newts belong to a group of animals called **amphibians**. Mammals such as water shrews may visit to hunt fish.

Adult newts mainly live on land, but lay their eggs in the pond. The young grow up in the water.

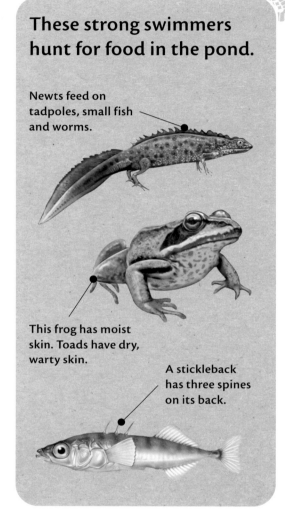

**These strong swimmers hunt for food in the pond.**

Newts feed on tadpoles, small fish and worms.

This frog has moist skin. Toads have dry, warty skin.

A stickleback has three spines on its back.

Tadpoles have a long tail for active swimming. Tadpoles are young frogs or toads.

Water shrews dive underwater to hunt fish, tadpoles, snails and insects. These little mammals are always hungry!

## What do you see?

Water shrews and voles live in burrows on the bank. Birds such as kingfishers live on the bank too. If you are quiet and patient, you may be able to spot the burrow-owner. Binoculars will help.

How can you tell frogs from toads?

# In and out of the water

Dragonflies are the pond's most spectacular insects. Their cousins, damselflies, are smaller but just as beautiful. Like frogs and newts, these insects grow up in water, and then the adults live on land.

Dragonflies grow up to 10 cm across. They can fly at 30 kilometres per hour! Damselflies are smaller and more delicate. Both catch flying insects which they crunch up in their toothed jaws.

## What do you see?

Adult dragonflies live by water and hunt flying insects. They are large and quite bold, so they are easy to spot. You can also look for cast-off dragonfly skins among water plants.

large, see-through wings

huge eyes cover most of the head

long body

In spring and summer dragonflies mate at the water surface. The male holds the female while she lays her eggs on plants.

Dragonflies may be bright red, green, blue or yellow. What colour are the ones you see?

The young dragonfly, called a nymph, grows up in the pond. When full grown, it crawls up a stem. Its skin splits to reveal the adult insect, which spreads its wings and flies away.

# Dabbling at the surface

When people think of ponds, they think of ducks. Some ducks feed by gobbling at the surface – a method called **dabbling**. Others dive down to the bottom. Both divers and dabblers are perfectly suited to swimming in ponds.

Mallards are the most common ducks. The female (right) has dull brown feathers. The male (below) is brightly coloured so he is easy to notice.

Can you tell the difference between the female and the male mallard ducks?

## What do you see?

Take breadcrumbs to the pond to watch ducks feeding. Soak some of the bread first. Throw the dry crumbs on the surface. Watch how the ducks feed using binoculars. The wet bread sinks, and some ducks will dive to get it. How long do they stay underwater?

Some ducks upend to feed just below the surface. Their waterproof feathers help to keep them dry.

Young ducklings take to water soon after they hatch.

19

# Among the reeds

Reeds and bulrushes grow by the water. These tall plants make it hard to see birds, frogs and other animals, but their calls may give them away.

Reeds and bulrushes grow up to three metres tall. They form a dense screen by the water.

This is a bulrush. The brown spike holds the seeds.

Can you identify the sounds you hear among the reeds?

The female mallard's brown, speckled feathers help to hide her while she is sitting on the nest.

## What do you see?

Birds, frogs and other animals can be identified by their calls. Frogs croak to attract a mate in spring. Ducks quack, while bitterns make an amazing booming sound. Curlews have a trilling call, while the coot's loud call sounds like its name.

Moorhens and coots live among the reeds. These birds can be easy to confuse, but the coot has a white patch above its **bill**. The moorhen, shown here has a red beak and yellow legs.

# At the lake

Lakes are large areas of fresh water. They are usually deeper than ponds and contain slow-moving water. Lakes have many amazing creatures. Long-necked birds feed by the water. Large fish such as carp, bream and pike lurk in the depths.

**Geese and swans have webbed feet. They are strong swimmers but walk with a waddle on land.**

These large, long-necked birds live by lakes.

A heron wades in the shallows and spears fish with its long beak.

A mute swan feeds on plants underwater.

A Canada goose eats waterweed, grass and seeds.

Herons, geese and swans all have long necks. How could this help with feeding?

Young geese and swans have fluffy, brown-grey feathers.

Adult mute swans have pure white feathers.

## What do you see?

Use your binoculars to study water birds. Make notes and sketches. Listen out for calls such as honks and hisses. Sunglasses will cut down reflections and help you to spot fish.

⚠ Lakes contain deep water. Be very careful near the edge.

# Life cycles

The best time to study pond life is in spring and summer, when animals have their young. Frogs, newts and insects pass through several stages in their life cycle. Birds such as swans take great care of their young.

The young swans, called cygnets, hatch after a month. They are able to fly four months later but don't get their white feathers until the following year.

Pond birds lay their eggs in spring.

⚠ Swans defend their nest and young fiercely. Don't get too close.

## What do you see?

Watch tadpoles growing up in the pond, or keep your own in a tank of pond water. Take just a small amount of spawn. Feed newly-hatched tadpoles boiled lettuce. Give older ones a tiny bit of dog or cat food. When tadpoles grow front legs, put them back in the pond.

Frogs lay masses of jelly-coated eggs in water. The eggs hatch into legless tadpoles. After about five weeks the legs start to appear. The tail shrinks and the animal becomes a tiny frog.

Frogs' eggs are called spawn.

This is an adult frog.

A tadpole's back legs appear first, then the front legs.

The legless tadpoles feed on **algae**.

How many different animals can you think of that grow up in water and then live on land?

Mayflies lay their eggs in water. The young (see page 11) spend up to three years growing up in the pond. As adults they live for just one or two days!

25

# Food chains

Living things in the pond form a web of life. As in other wild places, the rule is eat or be eaten. Plants provide food for **herbivores** (plant-eaters) such as worms, caterpillars and many insects. These in turn may be eaten by **carnivores** – meat-eaters such as herons and pike.

This grey heron has caught a frog. Frogs hunt insects such as flies.

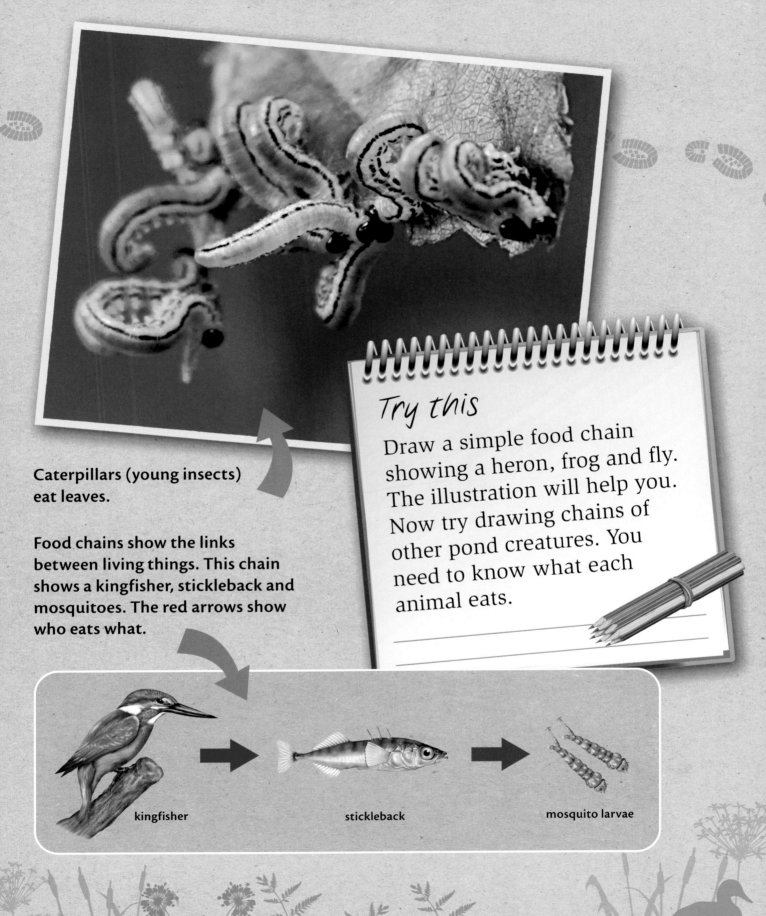

Caterpillars (young insects) eat leaves.

Food chains show the links between living things. This chain shows a kingfisher, stickleback and mosquitoes. The red arrows show who eats what.

**Try this**

Draw a simple food chain showing a heron, frog and fly. The illustration will help you. Now try drawing chains of other pond creatures. You need to know what each animal eats.

kingfisher

stickleback

mosquito larvae

# Nature diary

Ponds change a lot during the year. Spring and summer are the busiest time. Build up a detailed picture of pond life by keeping a diary. Building a small pond in the garden will help many kinds of wildlife.

## KEEP NOTES

**Always take your notebook with you. Note the date, time, weather and exact location. Describe and sketch what you see.**

This plant is called a flag iris. It produces yellow flowers in early summer and is found near ponds.

Date: 5 June
Time: 11am
Weather: Sunny
Location: Large pond
Observations: Saw a baby duck swimming and a family of geese on the bank.

Make a collection of finds such as feathers, and sketch leaves.

● Hide behind reeds, trees or bushes to get close to animals without being spotted.

● Listen for the calls of birds, frogs and other animals.

● Don't forget to look for tracks in the mud.

## MAKE A MINI-POND

Make a mini-pond in the garden using an old washing up bowl or better still, a small ready-made pond from a garden centre. Ask your parents where to put it. Dig a hole to match the shape and firm the earth around it. Put gravel and a couple of big rocks on the bottom. Add water plants in pots. Water creatures will soon move in!

In winter ponds and lakes may freeze over, and animals such as frogs are asleep.

29

# Glossary

**algae**  Tiny plants that live in water.

**amphibian**  One of a group of animals that live on land but lay their eggs in water. Frogs, toads and newts are amphibians.

**bill**  Another word for a duck's beak.

**carnivore**  An animal that eats meat.

**dabbling**  When a duck feeds at the surface by sucking water through its bill.

**gills**  The feathery structures that fish and some insects use to breathe underwater.

**habitat**  The natural home of a plant or animal, such as a pond, wood or meadow.

**herbivore**  An animal that eats plants.

**larva** (plural: larvae)  A young animal such as an insect.

**mammal**  An animal with hair on its body. Baby mammals drink their mother's milk.

**millpond**  A large pool of calm water.

**oxygen**  A gas found in the air and also mixed in water. All animals need to breathe oxygen.

**predator**  An animal that hunts other animals for food.

**webbed feet**  When an animal has skin between its toes, so that its feet work like paddles.

# Further information

## BOOKS

**Habitat Explorer: Rivers, Ponds and Lakes**
by Nick Baker, Harper Collins, 2006

**The Mud Pack: Wildlife**
by James Parry, The National Trust, 2002

## WEBSITES

**http://feeds.bbc.co.uk/wales/wildaboutnature/explorer.shtml?Rivers%20and%20Ponds**
BBC Wales Nature site has clips and information about pond life

**http://www.bbc.co.uk/nature/animals/wildbritain/gardenwildlife/myspace/content.shtml?24**
This BBC site gives more details about digging a pond.

**http://www.enchantedlearning.com/biomes/pond/pondlife.shtml**
Enchanted Learning is an American website which has a homepage about pond life.

# Index

# Nature Trail

**Contents of titles in the series:**

WAYLAND